365

Days of Inspiration from Japan

WHITE STAR PUBLISHERS

365

Days of Inspiration from Japan

CONTENTS

A NATION SUSPENDED BETWEEN

A unique kind of amazement and awe for Japan is discernible in the accounts written by the first Europeans to visit the remote island nation. European explorers first started coming to Japan in 1543. The grandeur of its military fortresses and the splendor of its houses, which were often embellished with "trees that would make nature jealous," the order and security guaranteed by its government, its effective educational system, its rich culture, and the sparkling cleanliness of its cities, led many explorers to call it "the best [civilization] that has been discovered so far." For once, Europeans found it difficult to feel superior to a culture outside the West. And unlike in the cases of so many other countries, Europeans did not turn into conquerors in Japan. Even their missionaries had to create a new playbook of evangelization methods, as they were acutely aware of the impossibility of "civilizing" a culture as ancient and complex as Japan's. The legacy left by this initial phase of contact (which lasted about a century) seems to have gradually dissipated as time marched on. This colonization extended slowly from insular southern Asia towards the east, setting the stage for a second encounter with Japan.

The Tokugawa shogunate in Japan had effectively ended the nation's seclusion, allowing contact with the outside world in 1854. In 1858, the country was

TRADITION AND MODERNITY

forced to sign the humiliating Treaty of Amity and Commerce with the United States to avoid war. Shorty afterwards, Japan signed similar agreements with the leading European powers. By this time, admiration for Japan and its culture was growing in France. This admiration was mainly centered on its art, including ukiyo-e paintings and woodblock prints. These pieces most likely came to the Netherlands first, beginning in 1854. Many Japanese ukiyo-e craftsmen began to acquire international audiences. Several were seen as artistic masters in the eyes of Western critics. In the works of painter and printmaker Hokusai, French art critic Philippe Burty (who later coined the term "Japonism") claimed to see the elegance of Watteau, the energy of Daumier, the imagination of Goya, the movements of Delacroix, and the sensitivity of Rubens.

From architecture to sculpture, engravings, calligraphy, and pottery, Japanese craftsmen and artists used entirely new approaches to portray nature and human interactions, opening up new horizons for artists and designers in the West. Items made out of wood, porcelain, and bronze, screens, kimonos, robes, and various everyday items were the subject of growing artistic and commercial interest in Europe, turning fashionable "Japonism" into the latest craze. These objects were beautiful and practical and an astounding combination of artistic richness, industry, and nature. To this day, many people prize Japanese products for their refined simplicity and elegance.

The legacy of this new, more intense phase of interaction between Japan and the West was substantial and lasting, as is demonstrated not only by the many magnificent Japanese art collections in Europe, but also by the view of Japanese culture that has prevailed in the collective European imagination. Japan's late-twentieth-century economic and technological progress has helped add further allure to its sublime yet mysterious capacity to balance tradition and modernity.

Westerners continue to be intrigued by the apparent contradictions of a country that, despite being situated well outside the "Western world," seems to resemble it the most. The Japanese writer Kenzaburō Ōe, who won the Nobel Literature in Literature in 1994, maintains that the West has a dual image of his homeland: one consisting of Samurai and Zen gardens, the other consisting of technology and efficiency. Suspended between these two images, he adds, is a void—the void in which Japan lives. And it is perhaps in this seemingly impenetrable void that the Western fascination with Japan also resides.

The images in this book are intended to explore this fascination. Each image is accompanied by bits of wisdom and creativity from Japanese poets, writers, and ancient Zen masters. Proverbs, poems, and maxims offer a glimpse into the Japanese soul while evoking a culture that seems at once close, familiar, inaccessible, and undecipherable. The images and text refer to an East in which the West, perhaps having lost its connection to nature and simplicity, will readily recognize and appreciate. They are meant to introduce you to forgotten times and faraway lands, the ultimate goal being to guide you into an emotional state in which you can successfully meditate on the present while dreaming of the future.

Rosa Caroli
Professor of Japanese History, Ca' Foscari University of Venice

1

January

Misty rain,
a day with Mt. Fuji unseen:
so enchanting.

– Matsuo Bashō

JANUARY

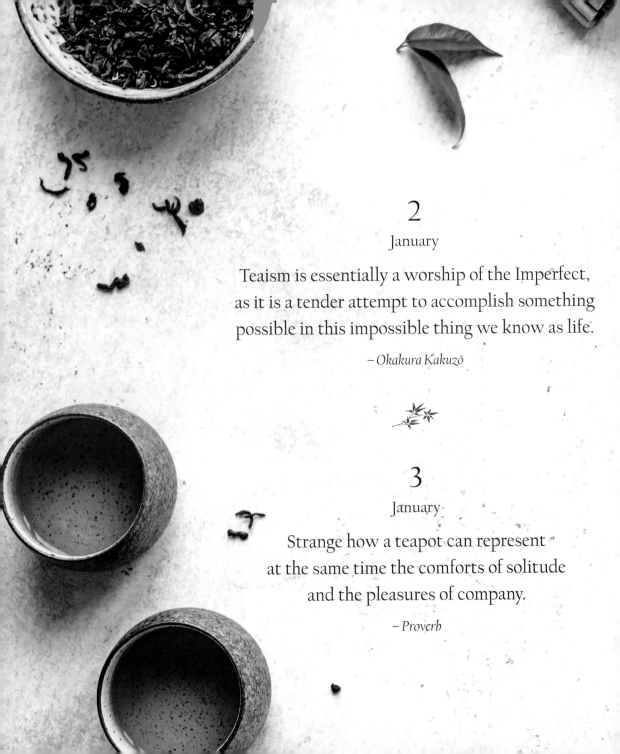

2

January

Teaism is essentially a worship of the Imperfect,
as it is a tender attempt to accomplish something
possible in this impossible thing we know as life.

– Okakura Kakuzō

3

January

Strange how a teapot can represent
at the same time the comforts of solitude
and the pleasures of company.

– Proverb

4

January

Behold with your eyes, listen with your ears.
Smell the aromas. Study assiduously and
acquire the spirit of tea.

– Sen no Rikyū

5

January

Do not seek to follow in the footsteps
of the men of old;
seek what they sought.

– Matsuo Bashō

6

January

It is the essence of the human heart not
to remain indifferent to what one sees.

– Akinari Ueda

7

January

One does not need buildings, money, power, or status to practice the Art of Peace. Heaven is right where you are standing, and that is the place to train.

– Morihei Ueshiba

8

January

Even dust if piled,
can become a mountain.

– Proverb

9

January

However you look at it, the human world is
not an easy place to live. And when
its difficulties intensify, you find yourself
longing to leave that world and dwell
in some easier one – and then, when
you understand at last that difficulties will
dog you wherever you may live,
this is when poetry and art are born.

– Natsume Sōseki

10
January

Anybody can be innovative
if his life depends on it.

– Akio Morita

11
January

Rituals are an external expression
of our inner state. We strengthen
and reinforce our inner state
by these external actions.

– Taizan Maezumi

12

January

A man sometimes devotes his life to a desire
which he is not sure will ever be fulfilled.
Those who laugh at this folly are, after all,
no more than mere spectators of life.

– Ryūnosuke Akutagawa

13

January

Without any intentional, fancy way
of adjusting yourself, to express yourself
as you are is the most important thing.

– Shunryū Suzuki

14

January

We find beauty not in the thing itself
but in the patterns of shadows,
the light and the darkness, that one
thing against another creates.

– Jun'ichirō Tanizaki

15

January

Fill yourself with the power
of wisdom and enlightenment.

– Morihei Ueshiba

16

January

The power we have to find all the difficulties in life helps
to make life easy for the majority of men.

– Yukio Mishima

17

January

Let me drop a word of advice for believers of my faith.
To enjoy life's immensity, you do not need many things.

– Ryōkan Taigu

18

January

Everyone has a spirit that can be refined,
a body that can be trained in some manner,
a suitable path to follow. You are here for no other
purpose than to realize your inner divinity and
manifest your innate enlightenment.

– *Morihei Ueshiba*

19

January

The temptation to give up is strongest
just before victory.

– Zen quote

20

January

The moon, snow, and flowers
cannot all be viewed
at the same time.

– Proverb

21

January

The heart of a human being is no different
from the soul of heaven and earth.

– Morihei Ueshiba

22

January

The Satori, enlightenment of Zen
Buddhism, is to live unconcernedly anytime.

– Masaoka Shiki

23

January

Curiosity is the key to creativity.

– Akio Morita

24

January

The emotions have no liking for fixed order.

– Yukio Mishima

25

January

Zen is not a particular state
but the normal state: silent,
peaceful, unagitated.

– *Taisen Deshimaru*

26

January

Cast off limiting thoughts and return
to true emptiness. Stand in the midst
of the great void. This is the secret
of the Way of a Warrior.

– *Morihei Ueshiba*

27

January

I think an understanding
of nature lies beyond the reach
of human intelligence.

– *Masanobu Fukuoka*

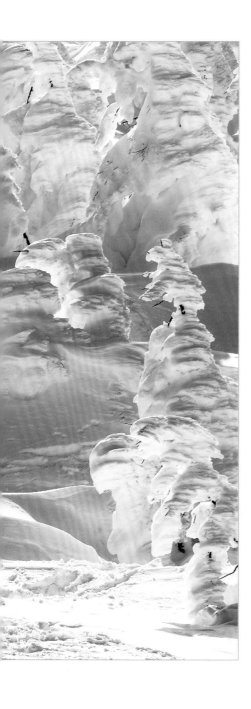

28

January

The quality that we call beauty
must always grow from
the realities of life.

– Jun'ichirō Tanizaki

29

January

Whatever you can conceive
or imagine is but a fragment
of yourself.

– Hakuun Yasutani

30

January

The Enso contains the perfect
and imperfect; that is why
it is always complete.

– Kazuaki Tanahashi

31

January

Things are not what they seem.
Nor are they otherwise.

– Daisetsu Teitarō Suzuki

1

February

Learn how to read the love letters
sent by the wind and rain,
the snow and moon.

– Ikkyū Sōjun

FEBRUARY

新潟県上越市上中田二七八
桜井市阿部七〇二
朱夢工房
静岡市葵区
㈱エクセレント・ライフ
代表取締役 佐藤 真知
愛知県高浜市
東京都福生市
大阪市北区
相和電気工業㈱
横浜市神奈川区
田中ミナ子
小林亜矢子
平成十九年十月吉日再々建
平成十八年六月吉日建之
平成二十七年八月吉日建之

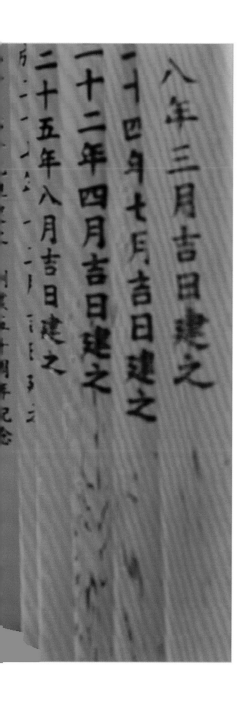

2
February

We meditate to make life meaningful. We must simply start with accepting ourselves. Meditation brings us back to actually who and where we are.

– Kobun Chino Otogawa

3
February

Zen is not some kind of excitement, but concentration on our usual everyday routine.

– Shunryū Suzuki

4

February

When man destroys the balance
of nature, the forest makes enormous
sacrifices to restore it again.

– Hayao Miyazaki

5

February

You must rise above
the gloomy clouds
covering the mountaintop.
Otherwise, how will you
ever see the brightness?

– Ryōkan Taigu

6
February

You grow old
when you stop learning.

– Proverb

7
February

Would that you might know
of my passionate love, deep
as mountain recess
where no call of flying bird
come to shatter the silence.

– Waka poem

8

February

Do not look upon this world
with fear and loathing.
Bravely face whatever the gods offer.

– Morihei Ueshiba

9

February

Matters of great concern should be
treated lightly. Matters of small concern
should be treated seriously.

– Yamamoto Tsunetomo

10

February

A willow tree never breaks
under the weight of snow.

– *Proverb*

11

February

The most precious thing in life
is its uncertainty.

– *Yoshida Kenkō*

12

February

There isn't a night that will not end.

– Proverb

13

February

Always keep your mind as bright
and clear as the vast sky, the great
ocean, and the highest peak,
empty of all thoughts.

– Morihei Ueshiba

14
February

In practicing meditation,
we try to realize what our life is.

– Taizan Maezumi

15
February

All beings by nature are Buddha,
as ice by nature is water;
apart from water there is no ice.

– Hakuin Ekaku

16

February

Perfection is everywhere
if we only choose to recognise it.

– Okakura Kakuzō

17

February

If you learn to enjoy waiting,
you don't have to wait to enjoy.

– Kazuaki Tanahashi

18

February

The Zen way of calligraphy is to write in
the most straightforward, simple way as
if you were discovering what you were
writing for the first time.

– Shunryū Suzuki

19

February

It is one life whether spent
laughing or weeping.

– Proverb

20

February

An object seen in isolation
from the whole is not the real thing.

– Masanobu Fukuoka

21
February

Like this cup, you are full of your
own opinions and speculations.
How can I show you wisdom unless
you first empty your cup?

– Nyogen Senzaki

22
February

Transiency is the naked
nature of time.

– Dainin Katagiri

23
February

Even people who seen to lack any finer feelings
will sometimes say something impressive.

– Yoshida Kenkō

24
February

If a man has no tea in him,
he is incapable of understanding
truth and beauty.

– Proverb

25
February

Tea has not the arrogance of wine,
the self-consciousness of coffee,
nor the simpering innocence of cocoa.

– Okakura Kakuzō

26
February

You cannot strike fire from flint
if you stop halfway.

– Nichiren Daishonin

27
February

A journey of a thousand miles
begins with a single step.

– Proverb

28/29

February

Green, green grows the spring willow.
But never plant it in your garden. Never pick
a falsehearted man for a friend. Although
the willow may bud early, does it hold up
when autumn's first wind blows?
A falsehearted man makes friends easily,
but he is a fickle. Whereas the willow
for many springs takes on a new color,
a falsehearted man will break off with you
and never call again.

– Akinari Ueda

1

March

Open your own door to truth.
Do not overlook the truth that is right
before you. The universe is our greater teacher,
our greatest friend. It is always
teaching us the Art of Peace.

– Morihei Ueshiba

MARCH

2

March

All of us, without exception,
are in the midst of the Buddha mind.

– Taizan Maezumi

3

March

It is like the lotus seed, which contains
both blossom and fruit.
In the same way, the Buddha
dwells within our hearts.

– Nichiren Daishonin

4

March

Purity is something that cannot be attained except
by piling effort upon effort.

– *Yamamoto Tsunetomo*

5

March

A major part of the world's goodness
lies in its unspeakable beauty.

– *Yukitaka Yamamoto*

6

March

So, if you have two pennies in your pocket,
buy one loaf of bread and one flower.

– Proverb

7

March

Poetry symbolizes the unshakable
stability of the world.

– Yukio Mishima

8

March

Life in this world is limited.
Never be even the least bit afraid!

– Nichiren Daishonin

9

March

Having an object that symbolizes freedom might make a person happier than actually getting the freedom it represents.

– *Haruki Murakami*

10

March

What is meditation?
Wisdom seeking wisdom.

– *Shunryū Suzuki*

11
March

The ideal teacher student relationship
exists when the student is better
than the teacher.

– Kenzaburō Ōe

12
March

The best way to attain Buddhahood
is to encounter a good friend.

– Nichiren Daishonin

13

March

Not fettered by desire by no means
offending anyone always quietly smiling.

– Kenji Miyazawa

14

March

Even though our path is completely different from the warrior arts
of the past, it is not necessary to abandon totally the old ways. Absorb
venerable traditions into this Art by clothing them with fresh garments,
and build on the classic styles to create better forms.

– Morihei Ueshiba

15
March

Do not wait until old age is upon you
before taking up religious practice.

– *Yoshida Kenkō*

16
March

Though worldly troubles may arise,
never let them disturb you.
No one can avoid problems,
not even sages or worthies.

– *Nichiren Daishonin*

17

March

Zen in its essence is the art of seeing
into the nature of one's own being.

– Daisetsu Teitarō Suzuki

18

March

Let us dream of evanescence, and linger
in the beautiful foolishness of things.

– Okakura Kakuzō

19

March

Even Fuji is without beauty
to one hungry and cold.

– Proverb

20

March

Shinto values nature and life.
This is because Shinto originally
arose from a sense of gratitude
and awe toward great nature.

– Motohisa Yamakage

21

March

We must embrace pain and burn
it as fuel for our journey.

– Kenji Miyazawa

22

March

The primeval man in offering the
first garland to his maiden thereby
transcended the brute.
He entered the realm
of art when he perceived
the subtle use of the useless.

– Okakura Kakuzō

23
March

So much I have learned:
the blossom that fades away,
its color unseen,
is the flower in the heart
of one who lives in this world.

– Waka poem

24
March

In joy or sadness, flowers are our
constant friends. We eat, drink, sing,
dance, and flirt with them. We wed
and christen with flowers. We dare
not die without them.

– Okakura Kakuzō

25

March

No matter how splendid in every way, there is something dreadfully
lacking in a man who does not pursue the art of love. He is, to coin
the old phrase, like a beautiful wine cup that lacks a base.

– Yoshida Kenkō

26

March

When meeting difficult situations,
one should dash forward bravely and with joy.

– Yamamoto Tsunetomo

27
March

You cannot separate any part from
the whole: interdependence
rules the cosmic order.

– Taisen Deshimaru

28
March

Which is more important . . . to be
successful, or to find some meaning
in your effort to be successful?

– Shunryū Suzuki

29

March

The circle is a reminder that each
moment is not just the present, but is
inclusive of our gratitude to the past
and our responsibility to the future.

– Kazuaki Tanahashi

30

March

Those who cannot feel the littleness
of great things in themselves
are apt to overlook the greatness
of little things in others.

– Okakura Kakuzō

31

March

Fifty today is better
than one hundred tomorrow.

– Proverb

1

April

Enlightenment is like the moon reflected on the water.
The moon does not get wet, nor is the water broken.
Although its light is wide and great, the moon is reflected
even in a puddle an inch wide. The whole moon and the entire
sky are reflected in one dewdrop on the grass.

– Eihei Dōgen

APRIL

2

April

No road is too long
in the company of a friend.

– Proverb

3

April

Have good trust in yourself, not in the One that you think
you should be, but in the One that you are.

– Taizan Maezumi

4

April

When you do something, you should
burn yourself completely, like a good
bonfire, leaving no trace of yourself.

– Shunryū Suzuki

5

April

We all have access to four treasures:
the energy of the sun and moon,
the breath of heaven, the breath
of earth, and the ebb and flow of the tide.

– Morihei Ueshiba

6

April

If there were no
cherry blossoms
in this world,
how much more tranquil
our hearts would be in spring.

– Ariwara no Narihira

7

April

To know your friends is to know
something beyond yourself,
beyond even your friend.

– Shunryū Suzuki

8

April

When we plot the happiness of another, we unconsciously impute to the other person what is in another form the dream in which our own happiness is fulfilled.

– Yukio Mishima

9

April

Seek freedom and become captive of your desires.
Seek discipline and find your liberty.

– Koan Zen quote

10

April

The dreamy feelings
when held between our fingers–
A butterfly.

– Yosa Buson

11

April

Friends are flowers in life's garden.

– Okakura Kakuzō

12
April

Going on a journey, whatever
the destination, makes you feel
suddenly aware and alive to everything.

– Yoshida Kenkō

13
April

When you ride in a boat and watch
the shore, you might assume that
the shore is moving. But when you
keep your eyes closely on the boat,
you can see that the boat moves.

– Eihei Dōgen

14

April

The heart that seeks something,
I release to the sea.

– Ozaki Hōsai

15

April

Not knowing how close the Truth
is to them, beings seek for it afar – what
a pity! It is like those who being
in water cry out for water, feeling thirst.

– Hakuin Ekaku

16
April

Preoccupied with a single leaf . . . you won't see the tree.
Preoccupied with a single tree . . . you'll miss the entire forest.
Don't be preoccupied with a single spot. See everything in
its entirety . . . effortlessly. That is what it means to truly "see."

– Takuan Sōhō

17
April

Teaism is the art of concealing beauty that you may
discover it, of suggesting what you dare not reveal.

– Okakura Kakuzō

18
April

Keep your hands open, all the desert sand
will pass through your hands. Close your
hands, you will get just few grains of sand.

– Eihei Dōgen

19
April

A strong man overcomes an obstacle,
a wise man goes the whole way.

– Zen quote

20
April

There is something
to be learned from a rainstorm.

– Yamamoto Tsunetomo

21
April

Spring rain–
all things on earth
become beautiful.

– Fukuda Chiyo-ni

22

April

A father's goodness is higher
than the mountain, a mother's goodness
deeper than the sea.

– Proverb

23

April

If you are self-centered, you spoil
everything, but if you are selfless,
everything goes smoothly.

– Taizan Maezumi

24
April

Yes, a poem, a painting, can draw
the sting of troubles from a troubled
world and lay in its place a blessed
realm before our grateful eyes.

– Natsume Sōseki

25
April

Progress comes to those who train
and train; reliance on secret techniques
will get you nowhere.

– Morihei Ueshiba

26
April

The wind howls,
but the mountain remains still.

– Proverb

27
April

Guided by a love
that has no bounds I shall go
to him by darkness–
surely no one will question
one who treads the path of dreams.

– Ono no Komachi

28
April

You will always exist in the universe
in one form or another.

– Shunryū Suzuki

29
April

To keep the proportion of things
and give place to others without losing
one's own position was the secret
of success in the mundane drama.

– Okakura Kakuzō

30
April

Don't be afraid to go slowly.
Be afraid of stopping.

– Zen quote

1

May

Shall we be alone
in enjoying these delights –
sweet cherry blossoms –
let us gather armfuls to
carry home as souvenirs.

– Hoshi Sosei

MAY

2

May

Unhappiness can be
a bridge to happiness.

– Proverb

3

May

Leave your front door and your back
door open. Allow your thoughts
to come and go.

– Shunryū Suzuki

4

May

The deepest love
is often hidden.

– Yamamoto Tsunetomo

5

May

All life is a manifestation of the spirit,
the manifestation of love.

– Morihei Ueshiba

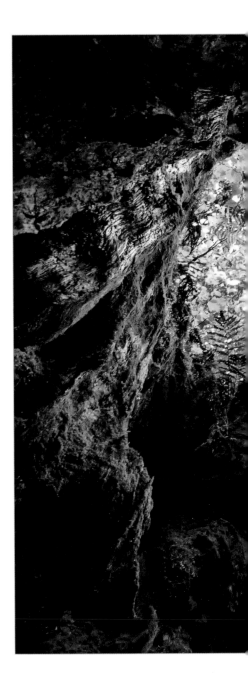

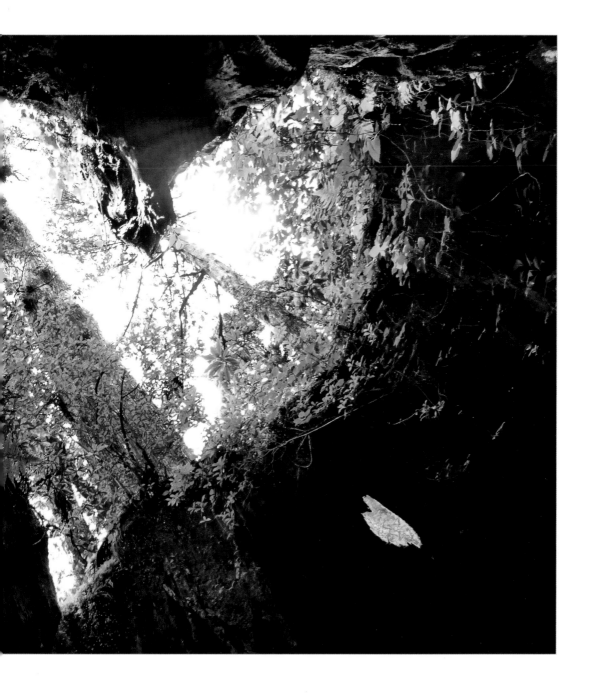

6
May

Is it freedom to follow one's ego, one's desires? It is to follow the cosmic order.

– Taisen Deshimaru

7
May

Having no destination,
I am never lost.

–Ikkyū Sōjun

8

May

Why is it impossible to know nature?
That which is conceived to be nature
is only the idea of nature arising
in each person's mind.

– Masanobu Fukuoka

9

May

Humans are not mere insensate
beings like trees or rocks, after all,
things can really strike home.

– Yoshida Kenkō

10
May

The moment that you are living right
now is a very important opportunity
to make your life vividly alive.

– Dainin Katagiri

11
May

Life at each moment permeates
the entire realm of phenomena
and is revealed in all phenomena.
To be awakened to this principle is itself
the mutually inclusive relationship of life
at each moment and all phenomena.

– Nichiren Daishonin

12

May

To study the self is to forget the self.
To forget the self is to be actualized
by myriad things.

– Eihei Dōgen

13

May

Always look on the bright side
of things. If you can't comprehend this,
polish that which has become dull
until it begins to shine.

– Zen quote

14

May

The future is losing what we have
today, and seeing something
we don't have yet arise.

– Ryū Murakami

15

May

There is no light for those
who do not know darkness.

– Takehiko Inoue

16

May

Bad intentions cannot travel
as far as good.

– Yukio Mishima

17
May

In order to comprehend the beauty
of a Japanese garden, it is necessary
to understand – or at least to learn
to understand – the beauty of stone.

– Lafcadio Hearn

18
May

Unspoken words
are the flowers of silence.

– Proverb

19

May

The thoughts that make you
inexplicably melancholy are those
that prove to be right.

– Kafū Nagai

20

May

This day will not come again.
Each minute is worth a priceless gem.

– Takuan Sōhō

21

May

In this world of dreams, drifting off still more;
and once again speaking and dreaming of dreams.
Just let it be.

– Ryōkan Taigu

22

May

A thing which fades
with no outward sign –
Is the flower
of the heart of man
in this world!

– Ono no Komachi

23
May

The greater one's pleasures,
the greater the pain. If you try
to sever the two, life falls apart.

– Natsume Sōseki

24
May

The Divine is not something high
above us. It is in heaven,
it is in earth, it is inside of us.

– Morihei Ueshiba

25
May

There's no limit
to things.

– Proverb

26
May

How bright and transparent
the moonlight of wisdom.

– Hakuin Ekaku

27
May

If you are unable to find the truth
right where you are, where else
do you expect to find it?

– Eihei Dōgen

28

May

The wisdom of the old is eternally
murky, the actions of the young
eternally transparent.

– Yukio Mishima

29

May

Have the fearless attitude of a hero
and the loving heart of a child.

– Soyen Shaku

30

May

Receive a guest with the same attitude you have
when alone. When alone, maintain the same attitude
you have in receiving guests.

– Soyen Shaku

31

May

The shallow is easy to embrace, but the profound
is difficult. To discard the shallow and seek
the profound is the way of a person of courage.

– Nichiren Daishonin

1

June

Our mind is the canvas on which the artists
lay their colour; their pigments are our emotions;
their chiaroscuro the light of joy, the shadow of sadness.
The masterpiece is of ourselves, as we are of the masterpiece.

– Okakura Kakuzō

JUNE

2

June

Cherry Blossoms
fall at the peak of their beauty
in this world to teach our hearts
to be free of attachment.

– Ōtagaki Rengetsu

3

June

The value of life can be measured
by how many times your soul
has been deeply stirred.

– Soichiro Honda

4

June

Salvation must be sought in the finite itself, there is
nothing infinite apart from finite things.

– Daisetsu Teitarō Suzuki

5

June

Life is the most precious of all treasures. Even one extra day
of life is worth more than ten million ryō of gold.

– Nichiren Daishonin

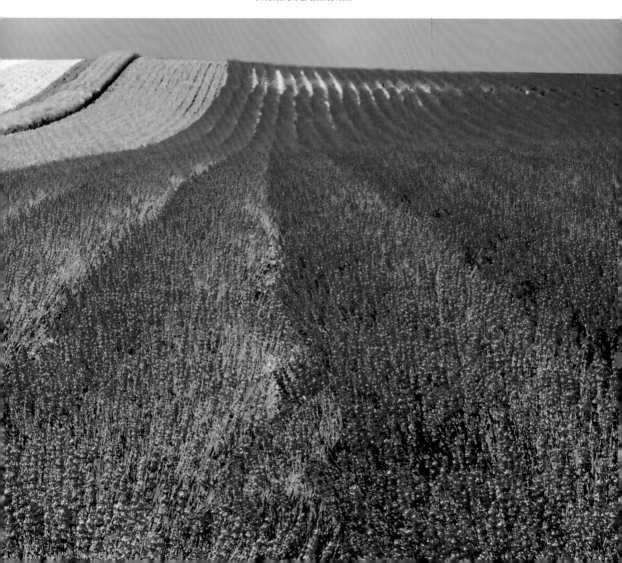

6

June

To receive everything,
one must open one's hands and give.

– *Taisen Deshimaru*

7

June

When we do not expect anything,
we can be ourselves. That is our way,
to live fully in each moment of time.

– *Shunryū Suzuki*

8

June

Being free always involves being lonely.

– Kōbō Abe

9

June

It's better be a person for a day
than to be a shadow for a thousand days.

– Zen quote

10

June

At the magic touch of the beautiful
the secret chords of our being are
awakened; we vibrate and thrill
in response to its call.

– Okakura Kakuzō

11

June

If you live even one day longer, you can
accumulate that much more benefit.
How truly precious your life is!

– Nichiren Daishonin

12

June

If a mirror had a color and a form
there would be nothing reflected.
It is emptiness that best contains things.

– Yoshida Kenkō

13

June

In a mad world,
only the mad are sane!

– Akira Kurosawa

14

June

Truth can be reached only through
the comprehension of opposites.

– Okakura Kakuzō

15

June

Trying to become someone else,
you lose your practice and lose
your virtue. When you are faithful
to your position or your work,
your true being is there.

– Shunryū Suzuki

16

June

Wabi-sabi means treading lightly
on the planet and knowing how
to appreciate whatever is encountered,
no matter how trifling,
whenever it is encountered.

– Leonard Koren

17
June

We don't practice to attain
enlightenment. We practice dragged
around by enlightenment.

– Kôdô Sawaki

18
June

Loving a heartless
unmerciful creature
I justify breathe laments
until the mountain echo
answers my piteous paints.

– Waka poem

19
June

There is nothing so easy to say
but so hard to do as give up.

– Santōka Taneda

20
June

There is no royal road to learning.

– Proverb

21
June

We ordinary people can see neither
our own eyelashes, which are so close,
nor the heavens in the distance.
Likewise, we do not see that
the Buddha exists in our own hearts.

– *Nichiren Daishonin*

22
June

Buddha is not divine.
Buddha is your daily life.

– *Taisen Deshimaru*

23
June

How quickly we forget our actions!
While the emotions in our memory
linger, our actions pass without a trace.

– Yukio Mishima

24
June

Because of the imperfect character
of ourselves we have to express our
inmost feeling through our imperfect
body and characters.

– Shunryū Suzuki

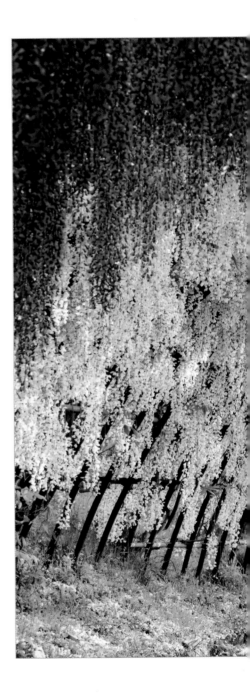

25

June

A lifetime is only an insignificant
interval in the endless flow of time.

– Eiji Yoshikawa

26

June

Our thoughts do not travel
to what we cannot see.
The unseen for us does not exist.

– Jun'ichirō Tanizaki

27
June

Matters that threatened to be difficult prove easy, while those that should be straightforward turn out to cause you great pains. The progress of each passing day is quite unlike your anticipation of it. And the same goes for a year – and for a life.

– Yoshida Kenkō

28

June

When time and space intervene, it is possible to be deceived by both, but on the other hand, it is equally possible to drive twice as close to her real self.

– Yukio Mishima

29
June

Don't stick to anything, not even
the truth. When you practice as though
this were your last moment, you will
have freedom from everything. Sit with
everything. Be one with everything.

– *Shunryū Suzuki*

30
June

Time flows in the same way
for all human beings;
every human being flows
through time in a different way.

– *Yasunari Kawabata*

1

July

Harmonizing opposites by going back to their source is
the distinctive quality of the Zen attitude, the Middle Way: embracing
contradictions, making a synthesis of them, achieving balance.

– Taisen Deshimaru

JULY

2
July

More valuable than treasures
in a storehouse are the treasures
of the body, and the treasures
of the heart are the most valuable of all.

– Nichiren Daishonin

3
July

There is meaning and basic satisfaction
just in living close to the source
of things. Life is song and poetry.

– Masanobu Fukuoka

4

July

All men are brothers, like the seas
throughout the world; so why do winds
and waves clash so fiercely everywhere?

– *Hirohito*

5

July

A frog in a well cannot conceive
of the ocean.

– *Proverb*

6

July

There is nothing that says more
about its creator
than the work itself.

– Akira Kurosawa

7

July

If a person hasn't ever experienced
true despair, she grows old never
knowing how to evaluate where
she is in life; never understanding
what joy really is.

– Banana Yoshimoto

8

July

When you fold, the ritual and the act
of creation is more important than
the final result. When your hands
are busy your heart is serene.

– Akira Yoshizawa

9

July

A person of wisdom is not one who
practices Buddhism apart from worldly
affairs but, rather, one who thoroughly
understands the principles by which
the world is governed.

– Nichiren Daishonin

10
July

The eyes speak as clearly
as the mouth.

– Proverb

11
July

If I were asked to explain
the Japanese spirit,
I would say it is wild cherry blossoms
glowing in the morning sun!

– Motoori Norinaga

12
July

Be present, from moment
to moment, right in the middle
of the real stream of time.
That gives you spiritual security.

– Dainin Katagiri

13

July

Suffer what there is to suffer, enjoy what there is to enjoy. Regard both suffering and joy as facts of life.

– Nichiren Daishonin

14

July

We don't know what will happen. If you fail to express yourself fully on each moment, you may regret it later.

– Shunryū Suzuki

15

July

Nirvana is right here,
before our eyes.

– Hakuin Ekaku

16

July

The art of life lies in a constant
readjustment to our surroundings.
Taoism accepts the mundane
as it is and tries to find beauty
in our world of woe and worry.

– Okakura Kakuzō

17
July

It is excellent for a man to be simple
in his tastes, to avoid extravagance,
to own no possessions, to entertain
no craving for worldly success.

– Yoshida Kenkō

18
July

Intrinsically all living beings are
Buddhas, endowed with wisdom
and virtue, but because men's minds
have become inverted through delusive
thinking, they fail to perceive this.

– Sutra Kegon

19

July

Zen is an extremely clear
and concise teaching.

– Sekkei Harada

20

July

If the sun and moon were not in the heavens,
how could plants and trees grow?

– Nichiren Daishonin

21

July

Even a false imitation of wisdom
must be reckoned as wisdom.

– Yoshida Kenkō

22
July

A flower does not think of competing
to the flower next to it. It just blooms.

– Zenkei Shibayama

23
July

When a man directs all his energies
into a single purpose,
nothing is impossible.

– Mori Ōgai

24
July

Light and dark are sides of the same coin; wherever the sun shines, shadows too must fall.

– *Natsume Sōseki*

25
July

Something born from human pride and the quest for pleasure cannot be considered true culture. True culture is born within nature, and is simple, humble, and pure.

– *Masanobu Fukuoka*

26
July

Moment after moment,
everyone comes out from nothingness.
This is the true joy of life.

– Shunryū Suzuki

27
July

We must remember that art is of value
only to the extent that it speaks
to us. It might be a universal language
if we ourselves were universal
in our sympathies.

– Okakura Kakuzō

28
July

Man is a genius when he is dreaming.

– Akira Kurosawa

29
July

At the bottom of great doubt
lies great awakening.

– Hakuin Ekaku

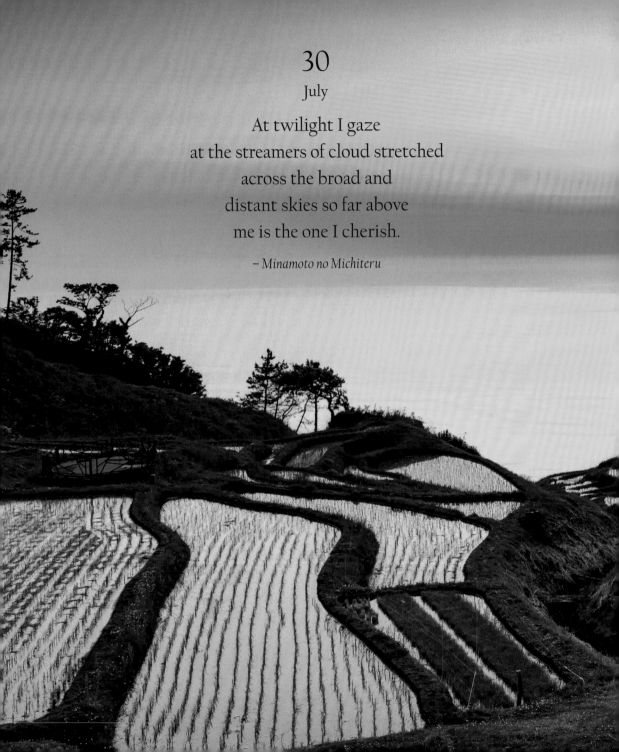

30
July

At twilight I gaze
at the streamers of cloud stretched
across the broad and
distant skies so far above
me is the one I cherish.

– Minamoto no Michiteru

31

July

You are at the very center of the universe – the very, very center of life itself. And so, if you yourself do not live tight, if you do not realize what this life really is, everything is spoiled.

– Taizan Maezumi

1

August

Each day of human life contains joy and anger,
pain and pleasure, darkness and light, growth and decay.
Each moment is etched with nature's grand design.
Do not try to deny or oppose the cosmic order of things.

– Morihei Ueshiba

AUGUST

2

August

To make a fortune some assistance
from fate is essential.
Ability alone is insufficient.

– Ihara Saikaku

3

August

You must exert yourselves
with all your might.
To realize perfect enlightenment,
you must let fall body and mind.

– Nyojo Zenji

4

August

When you become you, Zen becomes Zen.
When you are you, you see things as they are, and you
become one with your surroundings.

– Shunryū Suzuki

5

August

Failure is the key to success;
each mistake
teaches us something.

– Morihei Ueshiba

6

August

Fortune comes in by a merry gate.

– Proverb

7

August

The secret is just to say "Yes!"
and jump off from here.
Then there is no problem. It means
to be yourself, always yourself, without
sticking to an old self.

– Shunryū Suzuki

8

August

The ones who see true nature are infants.
They see without thinking, straight and clear.

– Masanobu Fukuoka

9

August

Your mind should be in harmony with the functioning of the universe;
your body should be in tune with the movement of the universe; body
and mind should be bound as one, unified with the activity of the universe.

– Morihei Ueshiba

10

August

Opposites carried to extremes come to resemble each other; and things that are farthest removed from each other, by increasing the distance between them, come closer together.

– *Yukio Mishima*

11

August

You should avoid the temptation of thinking that your dreams can be realized only in some far-off place. If you think that way, you'll neglect the possibilities in your immediate surroundings.

– *Eiji Yoshikawa*

12
August

How melancholy to think that your own familiar
things, too, will remain in existence down
the years to come, indifferent and unchanged.

– *Yoshida Kenkō*

13
August

Do not regret the past.
Look to the future.

– *Soyen Shaku*

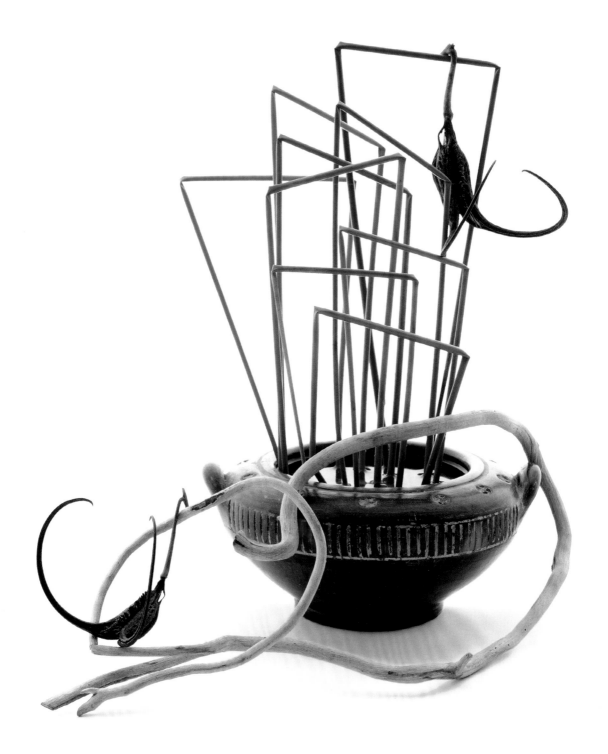

14

August

The sun became associated
with the main highway of my life.

– Yukio Mishima

15

August

If the minds of living beings are impure,
their land is also impure, but if their
minds are pure, so is their land.
There are not two lands, pure or impure
in themselves. The difference lies solely
in the good or evil of our minds.

– Nichiren Daishonin

16

August

Be grateful even for hardship, setbacks, and bad people. Dealing with such obstacles is an essential part of training in the Art of Peace.

– *Morihei Ueshiba*

17

August

Origami is a game that one plays with paper. There can be no more magnificent amusement than using hands in such a way that from fingertips birds fly, flowers bloom, and human figures come to life.

– *Kunihiko Kasahara*

18
August

There is a subtle charm in the taste
of tea which makes it irresistible
and capable of idealisation.

– Okakura Kakuzō

19
August

Human life is not sustained by its own
power. Nature gives birth to human
beings and keeps them alive.

– Masanobu Fukuoka

20

August

All day
I said nothing –
the sound of waves.

– Santōka Taneda

21

August

In this dream world
we doze
and talk of dreams –
Dream, dream on,
as much as you wish.

– Ryōkan Taigu

22
August

If you seek enlightenment outside
yourself, then your performing even ten
thousand practices and ten thousand
good deeds will be in vain.

– Nichiren Daishonin

23
August

Loyalty and devotion lead to bravery.
Bravery leads to the spirit of
self-sacrifice. The spirit of self-sacrifice
creates trust in the power of love.

– Morihei Ueshiba

24

August

Nothing is real except that which
concerns the working of our own minds.

– Okakura Kakuzō

25

August

Don't be afraid to make a mistake.
But make sure you don't make the same
mistake twice.

– Akio Morita

26
August

Contemplation within activity
is a million times better than
contemplation within stillness.

– Hakuin Ekaku

27
August

Our way is not to criticize others
but to know and appreciate them.

– Shunryū Suzuki

28
August

To the transcendental insight
of the Zen, words were but
an incumbrance to thought.

– Okakura Kakuzō

29
August

The point of the spiritual life
is to realize Truth. But you will never
understand the spiritual life, or realize
Truth, if you measure it by your
own yardstick.

– Dainin Katagiri

30

August

Do not chase those who leave,
and do not refuse those who come.

– Proverb

31

August

A man engaged in Buddhist practice
will tell himself at night that there is
always the morning, or in the morning
will anticipate the night, always
intending to make more effort later.

– Yoshida Kenkō

1

September

If your practice is good, you may become proud of it.
What you do is good, but something more is added to it.
Pride is extra. Right effort is to get rid of something extra.

– Shunryū Suzuki

SEPTEMBER

2

September

There is no better mirror
than an old friend.

– Proverb

3

September

If you win, the enemy will always be your enemy. But if
you persuade your enemy, he will become your friend.

– Morihei Ueshiba

4

September

Entering the village,
obey the village.

– Proverb

5

September

We can challenge each other
to a duel, win or lose. The strongest
are not those who live
the better life in this world.

– Takehiko Inoue

6

September

Even if you stumble and fall down,
it doesn't mean
you've chosen the wrong path.

– Zen quote

7

September

You must see with eyes unclouded
by hate. See the good in that which is
evil, and the evil in that which is good.
Pledge yourself to neither side, but vow
instead to preserve the balance that
exists between the two.

– Hayao Miyazaki

8

September

It is foolish to be in thrall to fame
and fortune, engaged in painful striving
all your life with never a moment
of peace and tranquillity.

– Yoshida Kenkō

9

September

The mind is the mountains, river, trees,
and grass, and the mind is the sun,
the moon, and the stars.

– Eihei Dōgen

10
September

Human beings are unable to be honest
with themselves about themselves.
They cannot talk about themselves
without embellishing.

– Akira Kurosawa

11
September

Always keep your body
filled with light and heat.

– Morihei Ueshiba

12

September

The conception of totality must never
be lost in that of the individual.

– Okakura Kakuzō

13

September

A good stance and posture
reflect a proper state of mind.

– Morihei Ueshiba

14

September

A moment
in life's brevity –
autumn sunset.

– Yosa Buson

15

September

If he cannot stop the mind that seeks
after fame and profit, he will spend
his life without finding peace.

– Eihei Dōgen

16

September

People sometimes work more than
they need to for the things that
they desire, and some things that
they desire they do not need.

– *Masanobu Fukuoka*

17

September

In this volatile world, things never go
according to our wishes.

– *Ihara Saikaku*

18

September

A hut full of laughter is richer
than a palace full of sadness.

– Zen quote

19

September

All faults derive from making oneself
out to be expert and at ease
with things, being smug,
and despising others.

–Yoshida Kenkō

20
September

Learn wisdom by the follies of others.

– Proverb

21
September

Every weakness contains
within itself a strength.

– Shūsaku Endō

22

September

Once you meet someone, you never really forget them.
It just takes a while for your memory to come back to you.

– Hayao Miyazaki

23

September

People distinguish between Self and Other. To the extent that the ego
exists, to the extent that there is an "other," people will not be relieved
from love and hatred.

– Masanobu Fukuoka

24

September

To move heaven and earth without effort
is a simple matter of concentration.

– Yamamoto Tsunetomo

25

September

If the current sinks,
it will rise again.

– Proverb

26

September

A man's heart is like
the autumnal sky.

– *Proverb*

27

September

Life and death are of supreme
importance. Time swiftly passes by
and opportunity is lost. Each of us
should strive to awaken. Awaken!
Take heed, do not squander your life.

– *Eihei Dōgen*

28

September

When real happiness is with you, it will encourage you
both in your adversity and your happiness. When you are successful,
you will enjoy the success, and when you fail, it will also be okay.

– *Shunryū Suzuki*

29

September

A cup of tea
poured for me,
fills my heart.

– Sumitaku Kenshin

30

September

Teaism is the noble secret
of laughing at yourself, calmly yet
thoroughly, and is thus humor
itself – the smile of philosophy.

– Okakura Kakuzō

1

October

In our lives we know joy, anger, sorrow, and a hundred other emotions,
but these emotions altogether occupy a bare one per cent
of our time. The remaining ninety-nine per cent is just living in waiting.

– Osamu Dazai

OCTOBER

2

October

I can't do anything;
My life of contradictions,
blown by the wind.

– Taneda Santōka

3

October

In the autumn wind
leaves of trees on the mountains
alter their color;
and the human heart, my love?
How will it go, I wonder.

– Hoshi Sosei

4

October

People will become your enemies if you become eminent too quickly in life, and you will be ineffectual. Rising slowly in the world, people will be your allies and your happiness will he assured.

– Yamamoto Tsunetomo

5

October

He who knows himself must be said to be the man of real knowledge.

– Yoshida Kenkō

6

October

In extreme situations, the entire universe becomes
our foe; at such critical times do not let your heart waver!

– Morihei Ueshiba

7

October

What we call "I" is just a swinging door which moves
when we inhale and when we exhale.

– *Shunryū Suzuki*

8

October

If you work by a reason, you grow
rough-edged; if you choose to dip
your oar into sentiment's stream, it will
sweep you away. Demanding your own
way only serves to constrain you.

– Natsume Sōseki

9

October

Which is harder: devising an unsolvable
problem, or solving that problem?

– Keigo Higashino

10

October

Big mind is something to express,
not something to figure out.
Big mind is something you have,
not something to seek for.

– Shunryū Suzuki

11

October

The greatness of a mind
is determined by the depth
of its suffering.

– Hayao Miyazaki

12

October

The Tao is in the Passage rather than
the Path. It is the spirit of Cosmic
Change, – the eternal growth which
returns upon itself to produce
new forms. It recoils upon itself
like the dragon, the beloved symbol
of the Taoists. It folds
and unfolds as do the clouds.

– Okakura Kakuzō

13

October

Each moment is a miracle
encompassing everything: the joy
and sorrow, the failure and success,
the disappointment and happiness,
the celebration and grief.

– Kazuaki Tanahashi

14

October

Anyone who falls in love is searching
for the missing pieces of themselves.

– Haruki Murakami

15
October

Whatever you do, just do it, without expecting anyone's help. Don't spoil your effort by seeking for shelter. Protect yourself and grow upright to the sky; that is all.

– Shunryū Suzuki

16
October

We must reflect on important matters, even when it's difficult.

– Kenzaburō Ōe

17

October

The incomprehensibility
of society is the incomprehensibility
of the individual.

– Osamu Dazai

18

October

If you want to take care of tomorrow,
take better care of today. We always
live now. All we have to do is entrust
ourselves to the life we now live.

– Dainin Katagiri

19

October

For studying Zen, one should have
quiet quarters. Be moderate in food
and drink. Cast aside all involvements
and discontinue all affairs.

– Eihei Dōgen

20

October

We nurse a conscience because
we are afraid to tell the truth to others;
we take refuge in pride because
we are afraid to tell the truth to ourselves.

– Okakura Kakuzō

21

October

It isn't the lack of money that makes you poor.
It's the lack of generosity.

– Osamu Dazai

22

October

Life is like a lamp, and food is like oil. When the oil is exhausted,
the lamp goes out, and without food, life will cease.

– Nichiren Daishonin

23

October

People who know the state of emptiness
will always be able to dissolve
their problems by constancy.

– Shunryū Suzuki

24

October

Dreams, memories, the sacred – they are
all alike in that they are beyond our grasp.

– Yukio Mishima

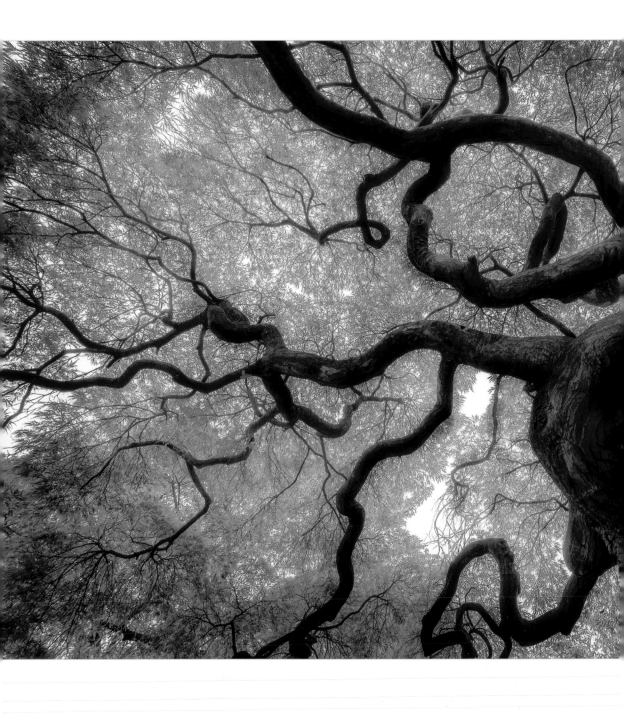

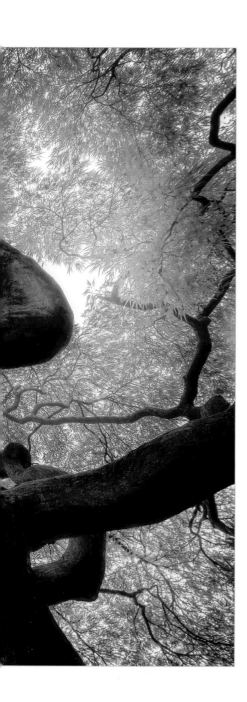

25
October

When a tree has been transplanted,
though fierce winds may blow, it will
not topple if it has a firm stake
to hold it up. Even a feeble person
will not stumble if those
supporting him are strong.

– Nichiren Daishonin

26
October

Egoism is a sin the human being
carries with him from birth;
it is the most difficult to redeem.

– Akira Kurosawa

27
October

Never cease forging your mind
and body to refine your character.

– Morihei Ueshiba

28

October

There's only one kind of happiness, but misfortune comes in all shapes and sizes. Happiness is an allegory, unhappiness a story.

– Haruki Murakami

29

October

The fundamental delusion of humanity
is to suppose that I am here and you are out there.

– Yasutani Roshi

30
October

Sincere repentance
will eradicate even fixed karma.

– Nichiren Daishonin

31
October

The changing seasons are moving in
every way. Everyone seems to feel that
it is above all autumn that moves
the heart to tears, and there is some
truth in this, yet surely it is spring
that stirs the heart more profoundly.

– Yoshida Kenkō

1

November

No one begrudges the passing moment.
Is this because they are wise,
or because they are fools?

– Yoshida Kenkō

NOVEMBER

2

November

To understand new things, study the old.

– Proverb

3

November

One may be letter-perfect in reciting the Lotus Sutra, but it is far more difficult to act as it teaches.

– Nichiren Daishonin

4

November

The mind of the beginner is empty,
free of the habits of the expert,
ready to accept, to doubt,
and open to all the possibilities.

– *Shunryū Suzuki*

5

November

The more you sense the rareness
and value of your own life, the more
you realize that how you use it,
how you manifest it, is all your
responsibility. We face such a big task,
so naturally we sit down for a while.

– *Kobun Chino Otogawa*

7
November

The moment between before
and after is called Truth.

– Dainin Katagiri

6
November

Carelessness is one's greatest enemy.

– Proverb

8

November

The idea that you can share anger or sadness with others is nothing more, really, than a compelling illusion.

– Toshiyuki Horie

9

November

Living without mistakes is truly impossible. But this is something that people who live by cleverness have no inclination to think about.

– Yamamoto Tsunetomo

10

November

When an opportunity comes do not let it pass you by,
yet always think twice before acting.

– Soyen Shaku

11

November

Every truth has four corners:
as a teacher I give you one corner,
and it is for you to find the other three.

– Koan Zen quote

12

November

All self-centered thoughts limit our
vast mind. When we have no thought
of achievement, no thought of self,
we can really learn something.

– Shunryū Suzuki

13

November

Something you want badly enough can
always be gained. No matter how fierce
the enemy, how remote the beautiful
lady, or how carefully guarded the
treasure, there is always a means
to the goal for the earnest seeker.
The unseen help of the guardian gods of
heaven and earth assure fulfillment.

– Eihei Dōgen

14

November

If you wish to be free of fault in all matters, be sincere
in whatever you do, polite to all, and speak little.

– Yoshida Kenkō

15

November

The reputation of a thousand years may be determined
by the conduct of one hour.

– Proverb

16

November

How very foolish
to make distinctions between
knowing and not knowing!
It is the devoted heart
that alone can serve as guide.

– Waka poem

17

November

Watch what you say,
and whatever you say, practice it.

– Soyen Shaku

18
November

By "error" I mean, quite simply,
taking your time over what should
be accomplished swiftly and rushing
into what should be dealt with slowly.
Regret fills you, but there is no
point in repenting now.

– Yoshida Kenkō

19
November

No blade can resist kindness.

– Proverb

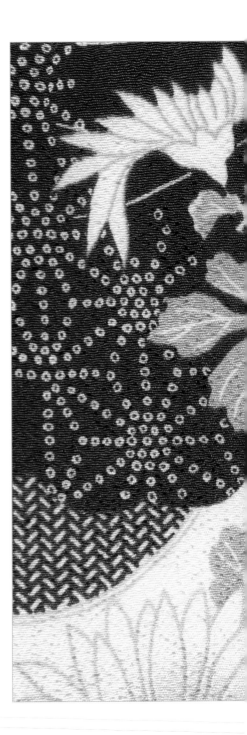

20
November

Gold can be neither burned by fire nor corroded or swept away by water, but iron is vulnerable to both. A worthy person is like gold, a fool like iron.

– Nichiren Daishonin

21
November

Those of us who know not the secret of properly regulating our own existence on this tumultuous sea of foolish troubles which we call life are constantly in a state of misery while vainly trying to appear happy and contented.

– Okakura Kakuzō

22

November

The past is all water under the bridge
and nothing can be done about it,
but it also lives on, implacably
creating the you of today.

– Teru Miyamoto

23
November

The day you decide
is your lucky day.

– Proverb

24
November

You may not be aware of the moments,
but as long as they continue to pass,
you will very soon find yourself
at the end of life. Thus, one dedicated
to the Way must not concern himself
over the distant future. His only care
should be not to let the present
moment slip vainly through his fingers.

– Yoshida Kenkō

25
November

The winds of tomorrow
will blow tomorrow.

– *Proverb*

26

November

A man who has never once erred
is dangerous.

– Yamamoto Tsunetomo

27
November

Think with your whole body.

– Taisen Deshimaru

28
November

If you must take care that your opinions
do not differ in the least from those
of the person with whom you are
talking, you might just as well be alone.

– Yoshida Kenkō

29
November

We learn little from victory,
much from defeat.

– Proverb

30
November

In all contentions there is neither right
nor wrong, neither good nor bad.
All conscious distinctions arise at
the same time and all are mistaken.

– Masanobu Fukuoka

1

December

What transforms this world is – knowledge.
Do you see what I mean? Nothing else can change anything in this
world. Knowledge alone is capable of transforming the world, while
at the same time leaving it exactly as it is. When you look at the world
with knowledge, you realize that things are unchangeable
and at the same time are constantly being transformed.

– Yoshida Kenkō

DECEMBER

2

December

Even if it seems certain that you will lose, retaliate!

– Yamamoto Tsunetomo

3

December

One kind word can warm
three winter months.

– Proverb

4

December

Sometimes it's as important to prove
there is no answer to a question as it is to answer it.

– Keigo Higashino

5

December

Defeat begins with
the fear that one has lost.

– Kōbō Abe

6

December

To live without hunger or cold, sheltered from
elements and at peace – this is happiness.

– Yoshida Kenkō

7

December

The person who admits ignorance shows it once;
the one who tries to hide it shows it often.

– Proverb

8

December

A good teacher is not one who never doubts, but rather one who strives to keep on learning despite the doubts in her mind.

– *Nahoko Uehashi*

9

December

By protecting others,
you save yourself.

– Akira Kurosawa

10

December

When someone knows something well,
it will not be seen in his manner.
This person is genteel.

– Yamamoto Tsunetomo

11
December

Fall down seven times,
stand up eight.

– *Proverb*

12
December

Sometimes you may feel you know
someone too well, and you have difficulty
appreciating them because of your small
mind. If you continue practicing together,
and your mind is big enough to expose
yourself and to accept others, naturally
you will become good friends.

– *Shunryū Suzuki*

13

December

A mind now clouded by the illusions of the innate darkness
of life is like a tarnished mirror, but when polished, it is sure
to become like a clear mirror, reflecting the essential nature
of phenomena and the true aspect of reality.

– Nichiren Daishonin

14

December

A samurai doesn't go back on his word.

– Proverb

15

December

An ethical man thinks of others first
and himself last.

– Kōbo-Daishi

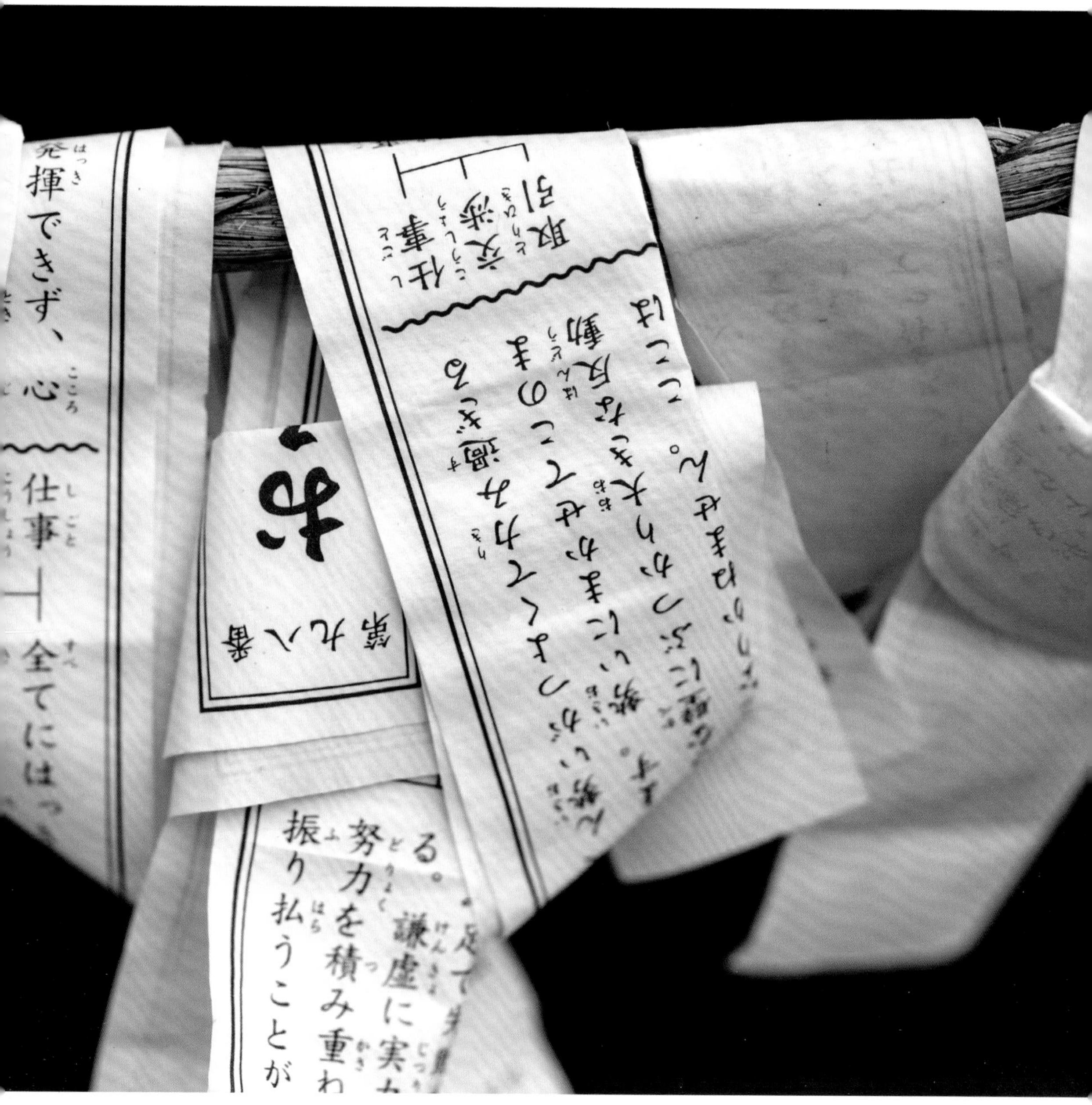

発揮できず、心

仕事

全てには

第○番

謙虚に実

努力を積み重

振り払うことが

16
December

If you forget yourself,
you become the universe.

– Hakuin Ekaku

17
December

Man was born for love
and revolution.

– Osamu Dazai

18

December

There is victory in losing.

– Proverb

19

December

And even though we say mind
and body, they are actually
two sides of one coin.

– Shunryū Suzuki

20

December

What we call the present is given
shape by an accumulation of the past.

– Haruki Murakami

21

December

Misfortune comes from one's mouth
and ruins one, but fortune
comes from one's heart and makes
one worthy of respect.

– Nichiren Daishonin

22

December

Asking a question is embarrassing
just for that moment. Not asking is
embarrassing and it will haunt you
for the rest of your life.

– Proverb

23
December

It does not matter whether one
is very smart or very stupid; there is no
distinction between those sharp and
dull faculties. Single-minded exertion
is itself pursuit of the Way.

– Eihei Dōgen

24
December

When one idea or thought arises, that
is birth. When one idea or thought
vanishes, that is death. Always there is
a constant repetition of birth and death.
This repetition continues through
past, present, and future.

– Sekkei Harada

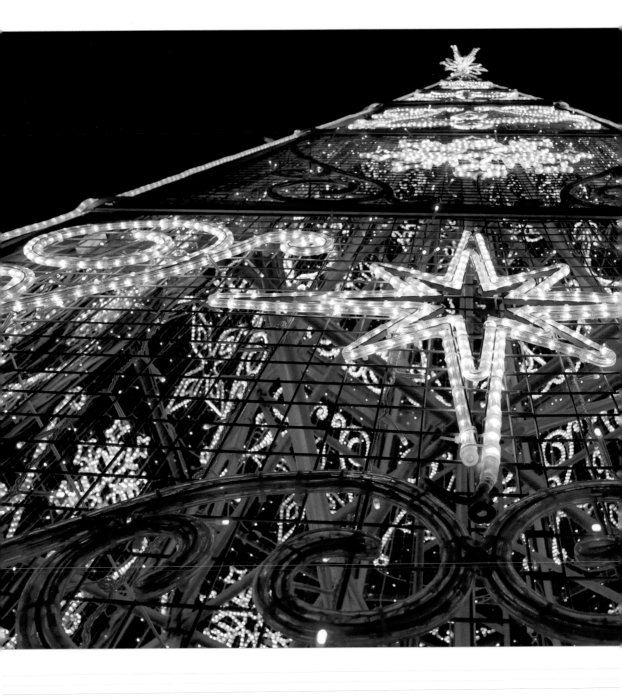

25

December

When you are not thinking that
you have another moment, then
naturally you can accept things as they
are, you can see things as they are.

– *Shunryū Suzuki*

26
December

If light is scarce then light is scarce;
we will immerse ourselves
in the darkness and there discover
its own particular beauty.

– Jun'ichirō Tanizaki

27
December

To sit alone in the lamplight with
a book spread out before you, and hold
intimate conversation with men
of unseen generations – such is
a pleasure beyond compare.

– Yoshida Kenkō

28

December

When you live completely in
each moment, without expecting
anything, you have no idea of time.
When you are involved in an idea of
time – today, tomorrow, or next year –
selfish practice begins. Various desires
start to behave mischievously.

– Shunryū Suzuki

29
December

In self-betterment, the word "end" doesn't
exist. He who considers himself complete
has turned his back on the Way.

– Yamamoto Tsunetomo

30
December

In the morning before dressing,
light incense and meditate.

– Soyen Shaku

31

December

One should become the master of one's mind
rather than let one's mind master oneself.

– Nichiren Daishonin

LIST OF CONTRIBUTORS

A

Akinari Ueda
(1734 – 1809)
Writer and *waka* poet, he is considered a prominent literary figure of 18th century Japan.
(January 6th, February 28th/29th)

Akio Morita
(1921 – 1999)
Japanese physicist and businessman, he was co-founder of Sony along with Masaru Ibuka.
(January 10th, January 23rd, August 25th)

Akira Kurosawa
(1910 – 1998)
Film director and screenwriter. He is regarded as one of the most important and influential filmmakers of the 20th century.
(June 13th, July 6th, July 28th, September 10th, October 26th, December 9th)

Ariwara no Narihira
(825 – 880)
Poet, he is appreciated especially for his *waka* poems.
(April 6th)

B

Banana Yoshimoto
(1964 – living)
Writer, one of the most appreciated Japanese authors in the Western world.
(July 7th)

Buson Yosa
(1716 – 1784)
Poet and painter, he is considered among the greatest poets of *haiku*.
(April 10th, September 14th)

D

Dainin Katagiri
(1928 – 1990)
Sōtō Zen *roshi*, he was founder and abbot of Minnesota Zen Meditation Center in Minneapolis.
(February 22nd, May 10th, July 12th, August 29th, October 18th, November 7th)

Daisetsu Teitarō Suzuki
(1870 – 1966)
Historian of religions and teacher of Buddhist philosophy, he was a popularizer of Zen Buddhism.
(January 31st, March 17th, June 4th)

E

Eihei Dōgen
(1200 – 1253)
Buddhist priest, he was the founder of *Sōtō* Zen school.
(April 1st, April 13th, April 18th, May 12th, May 27th, September 9th, September 15th, September 27th, October 19th, November 13th, December 23rd)

Eiji Yoshikawa
(1892 – 1962)
Writer, he is cited as one of the best historical novelists in Japan.
(June 25th, August 11th)

F

Fukuda Chiyo-ni
(1703 – 1775)
Poet of the *Edo* period, he is regarded as one of the greatest poets of *haiku*.
(April 21st)

H

Hakuin Ekaku
(1686 – 1769)
Buddhist monk and Zen master.
(February 15th, April 15th, May 26th, July 15th, July 29th, August 26th, December 26th)

Hakuun Yasutani
(1885 – 1973)
Sōtō roshi, founder of the *Sambō Kyodan* organization of Japanese Zen.
(January 29th)

Haruki Murakami
(1949 – living)
Writer and translator, his novels have been translated into 50 languages.
(March 9th, October 14th, October 28th, December 20th)

Hayao Miyazaki
(1941 – living)
Animator, filmmaker, screenwriter, author and manga artist.
(February 4th, September 7th, September 22nd, October 11th)

Hirohito
(1901 – 1989)
He was the 124th Emperor of Japan.
(July 4th)

Hoshi Sosei
(844 – 910?)
Monk and poet.
(May 1st, October 3rd)

I

Ihara Saikaku
(1642 – 1693)
Poet of the *Edo* period, he created the

floating world genre of Japanese prose.
(August 2nd, September 17th)

Ikkyū Sōjun
(1394 – 1481)
Buddhist priest, abbot and writer,
he is considered one of the most
eccentric Zen teachers.
(February 1st, May 7th)

J
Jun'ichirō Tanizaki
(1886 – 1965)
Japanese writer, he received the
nomination for the Nobel Prize
in Literature in 1964.
(January 14th, January 28th,
June 26th, December 26th)

K
Kafū Nagai
(1879 – 1959)
Author, playwright, essayist.
His works depict the life in early
20th century Tokyo.
(May 19th)

Kazuaki Tanahashi
(1933 – living)
Calligrapher, Zen teacher, he was author
and translator of Buddhist texts from
Japanese and Chinese into English.
(January 30th, February 17th,
March 29th, October 13th)

Kegon Sutra
Sutra of the *Kegon* school of Buddhism.
(July 18th)

Keigo Higashino
(1958 – living)
Writer, author of essays
and mystery novels.
(October 9th, December 4th)

Kenji Miyazawa
(1896 – 1933)

Poet, writer and agricultural science
teacher, he is regarded as the most
important Japanese author of
children's literature.
(March 13th, March 21st)

Kenzaburō Ōe
(1935 – living)
Writer, he won the Nobel Prize
in Literature in 1994.
(March 11th, October 16th)

Kōan Zen statement
Paradoxical story, dialogue, or question
which is used in Zen to provoke "the
great doubt" and help meditation.
(April 9th, November 11th)

Kōbō Abe
(1924 – 1993)
Writer, playwright, poet and theater
director. One of his novels (*The Woman
in the Dunes*) was adapted for a movie
which was nominated for the best
foreign language movie Oscar in 1964.
(June 8th, December 5th)

Kōbō-Daishi
(774 – 835)
Buddhist monk and artist,
he founded the Japanese
Buddhist School of Shingon.
(December 15th)

Kobun Chino Otogawa
(1938 – 2002)
Sōtō Zen priest.
(February 2nd, November 5th)

Kōdō Sawaki
(1880 – 1965)
Buddhist monk, he was one of the 20th
century's leading teachers of Zen.
(June 17th)

Kunihiko Kasahara
(1941 – living)
Famous origami master.
(August 17th)

L
Lafcadio Hearn
(1850 – 1904)
Irish, naturalized Japanese, journalist
and writer, his rendering of Japanese
legends and his ghost stories are
famous around the world.
(May 17th)

Leonard Koren
(1948 – living)
American artist and aesthetics
expert, he wrote several books
on Japanese culture.
(June 16th)

M
Masanobu Fukuoka
(1913 – 2008)
Japanese botanist and philosopher,
he was the pioneer of "natural
farming". (January 27th, February 20th,
May 8th, July 3rd, July 25th, August 8th,
August 19th, September 16th,
September 23rd, November 30th)

Masaoka Shiki
(1867 – 1902)
Poet, literary critic and journalist.
(January 22nd)

Matsuo Bashō
(1644 – 1694)
Poet of the *Edo* period, he is recognized
as the greatest master of *haiku*.
(January 1st, January 5th)

Minamoto no Michiteru
(1149 – 1202)
Waka poet and statesman. He served in
the courts of seven different emperors.
(July 30th)

Mori Ōgai
(1862 – 1922)
Writer, poet and translator
of the *Meiji* era.
(July 23rd)

Morihei Ueshiba
(1883 – 1969)
Martial artist, he was the founder
of *Aikidō*.
(January 7th, January 15th, January 18th,
January 21st, January 26th, February
8th, February 13rd, March 1st, March
14th, April 5th, April 25th, May 5th, May
24th, August 1st, August 5th, August 9th,
August 16th, August 23rd, September
3rd, September 11th, September 13th,
October 6th, October 27th)

Motohisa Yamakage
(1925 – living)
Shinto teacher.
(March 20th)

Motoori Norinaga
(1730 – 1801)
Writer and scholar of *Kokugaku*,
a school of Japanese philosophy
and philology.
(July 11th)

N
Nahoko Uehashi
(1962 – living)
Writer and anthropologist, author
of fantasy books and novels for kids.
(December 8th)

Natsume Sōseki
(1867 – 1916)
Novelist of the *Meiji* period, an era of
major political, economic, and social
change in Japan.
(January 9th, April 24th, May 23rd,
July 24th, October 8th)

Nichiren Daishonin
(1222 – 1282)
Buddhist priest, he developed the
teachings of Nichiren Buddhism,
one of the largest schools of Japanese
Buddhism.
(February 26th, March 3rd, March 8th,
March 12th, March 16th, May 11th,
May 31st, June 5th, June 11th, June 21st,
July 2nd, July 9th, July 13th, July 10th,

August 15th, August 22nd,
October 22nd, October 25th,
October 30th, November 3rd,
November 20th, December 13th,
December 21st, December 31st)

Nyogen Senzaki
(1876 – 1958)
Rinzai Zen monk, who was one
of the 20th century's leading
proponents of Zen Buddhism
in the United States.
(February 21st)

Nyojo Zenji
(13th century)
Buddhist priest.
(August 3rd)

O
Okakura Kakuzō
(1862 – 1913)
Writer, he was the author of
The Book of Tea that was the first
essay on the Japanese Tea
Ceremony written in English.
(January 2nd, February 16th,
February 25th, March 18th,
March 22nd, March 24th, March 30th,
April 11th, April 17th, April 29th,
June 1st, June 10th, June 14th, July
16th, July 27th, August 18th, August
24th, August 28th, September 12th,
September 30th, October 12th,
October 20th, November 21st)

Ono no Komachi
(825 – 900)
Waka poet, she was also renowned
for her exceptional beauty.
(April 27th, May 22nd)

Osamu Dazai
(1909 – 1948)
Japanese writer.
(October 1st, October 17th, October 21st,
December 17th)

Ōtagaki Rengetsu
(1791 – 1875)

Buddhist nun, potter and poet,
considered as one of the most
important poets of the 19th century.
(June 2nd)

Ozaki Hōsai
(1885 – 1926)
Poet, he witnessed the birth of the
modern free verse *haiku* movement.
(April 14th)

R
Ryōkan Taigu
(1758 – 1831)
Buddhist monk who is remembered
for his poetry and calligraphy.
(January 17th, February 5th, May 21st,
August 21st)

Ryū Murakami
(1952 – living)
Novelist, short story writer, essayist,
screenwriter and filmmaker.
(May 14th)

Ryūnosuke Akutagawa
(1892 – 1927)
Writer and poet, author of the novel
Rashōmon which inspired Kurosawa's
classic film.
(January 12th)

S
Sekkei Harada
(1926 – living)
Buddhist monk, Shike of *Sōtō* Zen
school, he is the foremost authority
of this school in Europe.
(July 19th, December 24th)

Sen no Rikyū
(1522 – 1591)
Zen Buddhist monk, he reformed the
Japanese "Way of Tea".
(January 4th)

Shunryū Suzuki
(1904 – 1971)
Zen monk and teacher, he is

renowned for founding the first Buddhist monastery outside of Japan, more precisely in California.
(January 13th, February 3rd, February 18th, March 10th, March 28th, April 4th, April 7th, April 28th, May 3rd, June 7th, June 15th, June 24th, June 29th, July 14th, July 26th, August 4th, August 7th, August 27th, September 1st, September 28th, October 7th, October 10th, October 15th, October 23rd, November 4th, November 12th, December 12th, December 19th, December 25th, December 28th)

Shūsaku Endō
(1923 – 1996)
Writer, who wrote from the rare perspective of a Japanese Roman Catholic.
(September 21st)

Soichiro Honda
(1906 – 1991)
Engineer and industrialist, he was the founder and the first president of Honda Motor Co., Ltd.
(June 3rd)

Soyen Shaku
(1860 – 1919)
Zen master, he was the first one to teach in the United States.
(May 29th, May 30th, August 13th, November 10th, November 17th, December 30th)

Sumitaku Kenshin
(1961 – 1987)
Haiku poet.
(September 29th)

T
Taisen Deshimaru
(1914 – 1982)
Sōtō Zen Buddhist teacher, he founded the International Zen Association.
(January 25th, March 27th, May 6th,

June 6th, June 22nd, July 1st, November 27th)

Taizan Maezumi
(1931 – 1995)
Zen Buddhist teacher and *roshi* (in Zen Buddhism *roshi* is used as an honorific title for a Zen master with a grade of great teacher).
(January 11th, February 14th, March 2nd, April 3rd, April 23rd, July 31st)

Takehiko Inoue
(1967 – living)
Manga artist.
(May 15th, September 5th)

Takuan Sōhō
(1573 – 1645)
Buddhist monk, he was a major figure in the *rinzai* school of Zen Buddhism.
(April 16th, May 20th)

Taneda Santōka
(1882 – 1940)
Poet of *haiku*.
(June 19th, August 10th, October 2nd)

Teru Miyamoto
(1947 – living)
Japanese writer.
(November 22nd)

Toshiyuki Horie
(1964 – living)
Literary critic and translator, teacher of creative writing.
(November 8th)

Y
Yamamoto Tsunetomo
(1659 – 1721)
Samurai and philosopher, he became monk in the old age.
(February 9th, March 4th, March 26th, May 4th, September 24th, October 4th, November 9th, November 26th, December 2nd, December 10th, December 29th)

Yasunari Kawabata
(1899 – 1972)
Writer, he won the Nobel Prize for Literature in 1968.
(June 30th)

Yoshida Kenkō
(1283 – 1350)
The most important writer of the *Kamakura* period (1185 – 1333).
(February 11th, February 23rd, March 15th, March 25th, April 12th, May 9th, June 12th, June 27th, July 17th, July 21st, August 12th, August 31st, September 8th, September 19th, October 5th, October 31st, November 1st, November 14th, November 18th, November 24th, November 28th, December 6th, December 27th)

Yukio Mishima
(1925 – 1970)
Japanese author, poet, screenwriter and essayist.
(January 16th, January 24th, March 7th, April 8th, May 16th, May 28th, June 23rd, June 18th, August 10th, August 14th, October 24th, December 1st)

Yukitaka Yamamoto
(1923 – 2002)
Guardian priest of the Tsubaki shinto shrine, one of the oldest shrines in Japan.
(March 5th)

Z
Zenkei Shibayama
(1894 – 1974)
Rinzai master well known for his commentary on the *Mumonkan*, a collection of kōans compiled in the 13th century.
(July 22nd)

PHOTO CREDITS

Introduction
Rosa Caroli

Edited
Studio Editoriale Brillante S.r.l.

Project Editor
Valeria Manferto De Fabianis

Graphic Designer
Paola Piacco

Editorial coordination
Giorgio Ferrero

WS White Star Publishers® is a registered trademark property of White Star s.r.l.

© 2020 White Star s.r.l.
Piazzale Luigi Cadorna, 6
20123 Milan, Italy
www.whitestar.it

ISBN 978-88-544-1666-6
1 2 3 4 5 6   24 23 22 21 20

Printed in Italy by Rotolito S.p.A. - Seggiano di Pioltello (MI)